this one time, at
Brand Camp

this one time, at Brand Camp

BRAND CAMP

ISBN 978-1-4357-5967-1

tomfishburne.com

Tom Fishburne
PO Box 1256
Alameda, CA 94501
tom@tomfishburne.com

to Tallie, Martha, and Charlotte,
my main squeezes

foreward by Jackie Huba

Brand managers can thank Neil McElroy for their jobs.

In 1931, McElroy was working in the advertising department at Procter & Gamble. He'd started in the mailroom and moved his way up, eventually being in charge of advertising for Camay soap, which then was a weak competitor to the Ivory soap juggernaut. Frustrated that his product lacked the budget and attention that Ivory received, McElroy had a Jerry Maguire moment: He wrote a memo. But McElroy's memo really would change the world. Well, the marketing world, at least.

In it, McElroy outlined a system that would give people inside P&G ownership for products. Each brand would have a dedicated budget and managerial team, and it would be managed as if it were a separate business. This way, brands could be built for different customer markets and, theoretically, would become less competitive with each other.

McElroy described a brand management team consisting of a "brand man," an "assistant brand man" and several "field check-up" employees. "Brand man." It just has a certain ring to it, no? It's practically a brand unto itself.

Even though McElroy's memo was a rule-breaking three pages long (one-page memos have been the rule there since the dawn of time), P&G's hon-chos adopted McElroy's ideas (and later made him president). McElroy's moment gave birth to modern-day brand management, a system that's been copied by product companies throughout the world.

McElroy might not recognize many of the issues worrying today's brand managers. Unrelenting price pressure from Wal-Mart. Television advertising effectiveness that's cratered under a fissured media landscape. Cheap competitors springing up virtually overnight. Vocal customers making or breaking new products on their blogs.

Thank goodness for Tom Fishburne.

Like McElroy, Tom is a pioneer. He takes the problems of the modern brand manager and their often absurd complexities and boils their essence down into the panel of a simple cartoon. Marketing people haven't had anything like him.

I've never been a brand manager during my career and being a fan of Tom's Brand Camp cartoons over the years, at least I know what they are going through.

Jackie Huba
Co-author, "Creating Customer Evangelists" and "Citizen Marketers"
Austin, Texas

big honking thanks

It takes a whole lot of happy campers to keep Brand Camp humming.

First of all, I'd like to thank all of my friends at method, Dreyer's (Nestlé), and General Mills, who have tolerated an embedded cartoonist in their midst. And lived in constant fear that something they said would be broadcast around the Internet.

Thanks to everyone who got me going on this cartooning adventure in the first place, including Prash Argawal, Professors Frances X. Frei and Stephan Thomke, and all of the bees in Section B.

Thanks to some of my cartoonist friends who have offered important encouragement along the way, including T. Lewis and Greg Kopervas, and my kindred spirit David t Jones, brilliant cartoonist of Ad Land.

Thanks to all the bloggers who have been incredibly supportive in the blogosphere, including Jackie Huba, David Taylor, Paul Williams, Seth Godin, John Moore, John Grant, and Chris Wilson.

Thanks to some cartooning patrons who gave some nice support over the years, including Mark Addicks, Joan Holleran, Jim Lawrence, Eric Ryan, and Hugh Burkitt.

And a big thanks to all of the Brand Camp readers out there, particularly the ones who take the time to write me.

But, most of all, thanks to my fabulous wife, Tallie, for being my cartoon sounding board, collaborator, editor, coach, reviewer, friend, advisor, accountant, conspirator, ego-stroker, sales rep, muse, and consoler continuously all these years. She makes oh so much happen to allow me to doodle as a hobby. And she's also quite understanding about the occasional India ink stain around the house. Sorry about those.

everything I need to know about marketing, I learned by drawing cartoons

This one time, at General Mills, I started a cheeky cartoon about marketing.

I created it mainly for my coworkers. We had all started learning the marketing ropes together. Important stuff like: how to pretend that our forecasts were any more accurate than fingers in the wind, how to blame the agency, and how to run Nielsen reports until our contact lenses dried up.

It felt like camp. So I called it Brand Camp, tacked a few rough cartoons onto my cubicle, and emailed them to my fellow campers.

And then I discovered that the camp was quite a bit bigger than I originally thought. I started getting emails from all over the world. It turned out that marketing soap in India and cell phones in Ireland has a lot in common with marketing yogurt in Minnesota. We all share the same inside jokes.

From an email to 20 friends in 2002, Brand Camp has grown purely by word-of-mouth to reach nearly 10,000 readers each week from companies and campuses around the world. Since then, I'm moved on from General Mills to Dreyer's (Nestlé) and then to method. And from the US to the UK. But the humor is the same.

I knew that my day job in marketing would provide cartoon fodder for my night job at the drafting table. What I didn't expect was that the act of creating a weekly cartoon would actually make me a better marketer.

So, in true camp spirit, here's some of what I learned at Brand Camp (other than how to short-sheet a bed).

find your niche

If you think of cartooning as a category, it's dominated by the mainstream newspaper. The newspaper comics page is shrinking in space, filled by a few strips that haven't changed much in decades, and impossible to break into. Sound like the grocery aisle?

By appealing to everyone, though, these cartoons are not that appealing to anyone in particular. Garfield scarfing lasagna may be mildly entertaining to the vast majority, but it's not screamingly funny to anyone.

I think this is why there is an opportunity for a cartoon targeted to the improbable audience of brand managers. Chris Anderson writes all about this effect in a book called "The Long Tail". The Internet allows my very niche sense of humor to reach pockets of niche readers all over the world.

Many brands dismiss niche markets in order to chase the mainstream. At one previous brand, we used to joke that our target consumer was a "woman, age 25 to 39, with a pulse."

But, I learned it is far more valuable to light a real fire with a small but loyal few, than to generally appeal to no one in particular.

attract not promote

From Seth Godin's "Purple Cow", I learned that it's always better to invest more in making your product remarkable than to invest in advertising a mediocre product.

Or, as Geek Squad founder Robert Stephens put it, "advertising is a tax for having an unremarkable product."

The only "advertising" I ever did for Brand Camp was my original email to a handful of friends six years ago. From there, it grew purely by people forwarding it around. It proved to me that good ideas can catch hold on their own merit. And that I need to constantly work at drawing cartoons people like to read, and the audience will come.

This discipline comes in handy working with a small brand like method. Our competitors literally spend more on employee toilet paper than we do on advertising. We're forced by necessity to make our products more remarkable, because we're fundamentally outspent (or undertaxed).

start conversations

I get lots of nice emails from Brand Camp readers. A brand manager in Sydney with a cartoon idea, a consumer insights manager in Minneapolis telling me I'm being too cynical, and a creative director in London venting about a client.

These emails give me cartoon fodder, help steer my topics in the right direction, and keep my finger on the pulse of what is going on.

Think about the average brand. A consumer call center typically employs some of the least paid and least in-the-loop employees in the company (if they're actually "in the company" at all). This is a missed opportunity considering that those who answer the phone are on the front lines with consumers who actually care enough about your brand to pick up the phone to call you.

There's a smoothie brand in Europe called innocent that has a banana phone in their office (literally a phone shaped like a banana). In the early days, it would ring with every single consumer call, and anyone in the company could fight over the privilege to answer it. Now that they're bigger, everyone takes turns at the banana phone.

Why don't more companies have a banana phone? I can't think of a better way to see how our message is resonating and to actually connect with consumers. And to remind everyone that we all work in marketing (even if your actual business card reads accounts payable or supply chain planning).

read the tea leaves (but don't drink them)

After I draw a cartoon, I usually have no instinctive idea if it's funny. Honestly. I'm too close to it. The only surefire way I can tell when a cartoon strikes a chord or bombs is from objective data.

I can tell by the number of new subscribers and blog hits how much each cartoon was shared. It helps me focus on certain themes (like sustainability) and ditch others (like sensory science).

It may sound geeky, but I can chart the numbers for every cartoon I've ever drawn to understand which ones are truly popular, which ones are polarizing, and which ones are humdrum.

Cartooning is mainly a right-brain activity, but I find this data essential to make sure that my cartoons resonate. For me, drawing cartoons is not just the fun of drawing them, but the interaction with people who like to read them. I can't go with gut instinct alone.

But, I find that the moment I start obsessing over the numbers, I lose my sense of humor. Good numbers happen when I'm focused on the cartoons, not the numbers themselves.

It's exactly the same with brand analytical data for me. I absolutely need data to know how my business is trending, but baseline volume fluctuates each week. The long-term health is important. The weekly ebb and flow is not. When I start stressing why baseline numbers are down one particular week, I stop planning creatively to grow my business in the long run.

always keep a sketch pad handy

Cartoon ideas are unruly. They come in the shower, on a run, and in the middle of a meeting when I'm supposed to be paying attention to something else. I've given up trying to contain them. I now keep a sketch pad handy and doodle when the inspiration strikes (while still trying to look serious and attentive in the meeting).

The worst experience for me is when my Sunday cartoon deadline hits and I don't already have an idea percolating. I can usually sweat out a cartoon idea in time, but it's seldom very good.

Likewise, I've found that I can't shoehorn business idea generation into a tidy box (like scheduling a half-hour ideation before a forecasting meeting or cramming new product brainstorming into a few weeks a year). The best ideas will snub my planning and play hooky.

In our office, we installed a floor-to-ceiling magnetic whiteboard we call the "wiki wall", where everyone in the company can jot down ideas, at all times. Ideas continually build on each other, and it becomes the foundation of our new product development. When the deadline arrives, we have a few that are already ripe on the vine.

In this book, I'm sharing more than three years of Brand Camp cartoons that echo some of these themes. Like any diary, this collection mirrors what was on my mind any particular week. So, I've included some running commentary to give some context and insight into each one.

I hope these cartoons ring true and show how much we all have in common. Please email tom@tomfishburne.com or go to tomfishburne.com with any thoughts or cartoon ideas (or care packages filled with brownies).

Enjoy!

Tom Fishburne
Richmond-upon-Thames, England
July 14, 2008

January 24, 2005

I always loved the movie Strange Brew when the McKenzie brothers try to cop free Elsinore beer by showing up to the factory with a mouse in the bottle.

When I worked on Yoplait, we kept getting calls from parents who had heard a rumor that we used bugs as an ingredient. I chuckled about this until I learned that the coloring agent, carmine, is actually made from boiling crushed beetles. Yum.

The funniest call, however, was from someone who actually found a Snickers wrapper in a bag of Green Giant frozen peas.

Tom Fishburne

February 14, 2005

If you work in a large company, you get used to rogue requests from the executive wing. They usually flow layer by layer down to the bottom of the chain. I once received an email request that had been forwarded successively five times until it reached my desk. And I was the end of the line.

It reminded me a bit of the hazing rituals in fraternities and the classic Kevin Bacon line in Animal House, "thank you, sir, may I have another?"

March 7, 2005

I drew this cartoon when transfat was under the magnifying glass, big time. Transfat went from being just another name on the ingredient declaration to public enemy number one. Every food brand I knew that had transfat were frantically reformulating to remove them. Those that didn't were frantically adding "no transfat" package claims. It reminded me a bit of the Hester Prynne treatment.

Tom Fishburne

March 21, 2005

This is a constant tension in making products that have "mass appeal". You can so easily create something that is broadly appealing to a large group of people but not really that meaningful to anyone in particular. Somewhere along the way, I heard one of these products described as a Swiss Army Knife. Those little foldable scissors may be cute, but they sure don't work as well as regular scissors.

March 28, 2005

Slotting fees have always mystified me. Retailers request massive fees just to list a new product. I know it's all part of the negotiation and helps lower some of the risk for the retailer, but it seems to stifle innovation, particularly for smaller brands. I'd much rather use that money for something that actually drives sales.

Tom Fishburne

April 12, 2005

Marketing lingo often cracks me up. I like the term "evangelist", but it always makes me think of the door-to-door pamphlet-thumpers.

April 26, 2005

I love plays on words. Often I get a cartoon idea just from the title, like this one or "Brand Identity Crisis" or "One Night Brand".

I love the simplicity of IZZE. Bacos was a nod to my timing on Green Giant, when the guy managing Bacos sat next to me. It just cracked me up to think of Bacos at a sampling event.

May 16, 2005

I once heard the Saatchi & Saatchi CEO, Kevin Roberts, give a talk on "lovemarks", which he defined as "loyalty beyond reason." He said that lovemarks inspire love and respect, brands inspire respect but not love, fads inspire love but not respect, and products inspire neither love nor respect. Kind of a handy framework.

Every brand I've worked on has talked about loyalty as this holy grail, but so much consumer loyalty with brands is pretty fickle.

June 6, 2005

This is a big watch word in focus groups. The moment a consumer says "special occasions", it means trouble, because they might like it in theory, but they won't buy it regularly. Our office shorthand for these types of concepts are that they would be "great for camping" (consumed only once in a blue moon).

This particular cartoon came after a round of ice cream flavor tests, with a really rich flavor that everyone absolutely loved for the first bite, but not for the whole bowl.

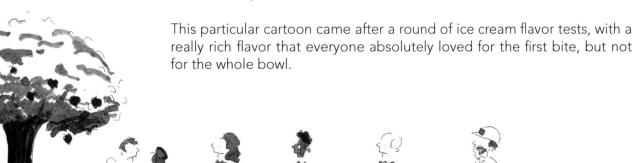

June 20, 2005

When I drew this cartoon, I was working with the Food Network on a reality show for Häagen-Dazs and they really wanted to film in the factory. I love factories, but if you ever tour one, you see all of the bulk ingredients lying around in massive totes. It kind of kills the premium cache to see products reduced to its commodity components. We had to be careful about what was filmed so that it still looked premium. Somehow that process inspired this cartoon.

July 4, 2005

I drew a lot of low-carb cartoons in the midst of the rush to launch low-carb products. Every brand I knew had low-carb projects in the hopper, most on an accelerated time line just to jump on the bandwagon.

We had a big company debate on whether it was a "fad" or a "trend". The answer, predicted our research group, was a "trad", which meant it had the suddenness of a fad, but the longevity of a trend.

Just a year later, the bubble popped, and it reminded me of my time in San Francisco in early 2000.

Tom Fishburne

July 11, 2005

I was invited to give a cartoon talk on food marketing at a conference, and sent a note out to Brand Camp readers asking for their perspective on the hottest topics in food marketing. They came back with a ton of ideas, and for the next few weeks, my cartoons became really "foodie" as I got ready for the conference. This nutraceutical one came first.

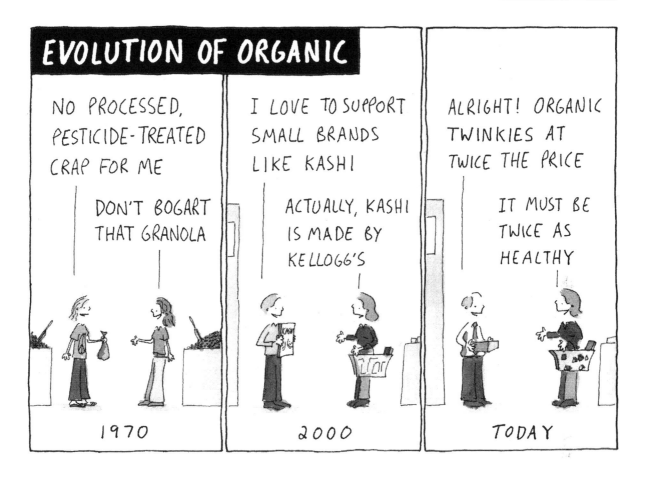

August 1, 2005

Organic is one of those claims that had been stretched and tweaked to where it loses some of its meaning. There has been a rush by brands to launch organic versions of its regular selves, and organic has been extended to other categories like personal care where it's not as relevant and largely unregulated. One of its perceived benefits is "health", which extends even to products with an unhealthy ingredient deck. This cartoon came after seeing a bag of organic Cheetos.

Tom Fishburne

August 15, 2008

This was another one for the food conference. Glycemic Index (GI) was a hot topic, but actually incredibly complex. A lot of foods you would think are good are not, and vice-versa. I was skeptical that it would ever take hold because of its complexity, and was surprised to see so many "Low GI" foods when I later moved to the UK.

August 29, 2005

This cartoon came after seeing a spate of foods claiming to burn more fat and cut cholesterol. Yet, every food scientist I knew recommended simple diet and exercise as the only real answer. It's a good symbiotic relationship. Consumers want a quick fix and brands can find a premium if they offer something that is perceived as giving them one.

Tom Fishburne

September 5, 2005

This cartoon was inspired by Jackie Huba, co-author of "Creating Customer Evangelists" and "Citizen Marketers" (who kindly wrote the forward for this book). Jackie was off to speak at a Word of Mouth Marketing Association Conference and thought that a cartoon might spark conversation. I later used this one as my inaugural cartoon in Brandweek.

It looks better with the bottle in color (see the back cover), which is modeled after IZZE, a brand I like.

September 19, 2005

I spent a bit of time doing kid marketing with yogurt, and we always talked about "kid nag". We had a chart showing degrees of "kid nag", with ice cream at the pinnacle. Our goal was to create as much "kid nag" with yogurt as with ice cream. This was while my wife was pregnant, but before I knew "kid nag" first-hand. I drew this cartoon when my "kid nag" karma finally came home to roost.

October 10, 2005

I have a lot of nostalgia for Schoolhouse Rock, particularly "I'm just a Bill". We got the DVD set for my daughters, and seeing the process of making a bill into a law reminded me of the Stage Gate product development process. Except Stage Gate can seem even more convoluted and political.

October 24, 2005

I've seen Frankenconcept happen again and again, particularly when there's urgency to have a new product by the next launch window. Often the new product pipeline will have a couple half-baked ideas, but nothing that is really ready to go.

Tom Fishburne

November 7, 2005

I enjoy reading psychographic profiles and the names the profile companies come up with are really clever. I do think it's interesting to see which profiles are more likely to buy which brands. This cartoon was inspired after a meeting with one of these profile companies. They had taken our postal codes in advance, and told each of us in the room what our profiles would be. The "urban elite" in the room felt really smug.

November 14, 2005

This cartoon was inspired by looking at the Low Carb detritus that had been discontinued and the No Sugar Added launches that were about to take its place. It felt like we were moving from one bandwagon to the next. And, of course, every new launch involved massive slotting fees to the retailers.

I was working with a few seasonal items, where the flavors would change every quarter but it was virtually the same product. These flavor changes seemed as temporal as the major food trends we were chasing.

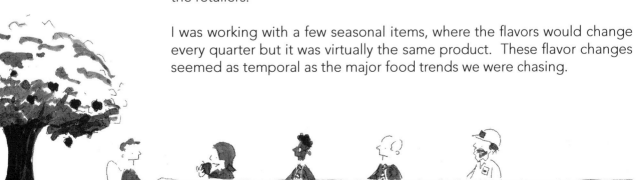

Tom Fishburne

November 28, 2005

I went to the Effie advertising awards in New York, and was struck by all of the glitz and peacocking of the black tie event. There were some other media examples there, but most of the attention was given to TV advertising.

At the same time, TV media (particularly the 30-second-spot) was really starting to lose its way. This cartoon was inspired by the contrast between the sad state of TV media and the hero status TV advertising once had. It reminded me of "Requiem for a Heavyweight", about a washed-up boxer who has been beaten by a younger fighter.

December 12, 2005

I first experienced "feature creep" when I was building web sites at an interactive agency ten years go (which is why I now have a lot of sympathy for agencies). We'd all agree to a project scope with solemn vows, and then slowly but surely add completely new features over the course of the project. Each one alone isn't such a big deal, but taken together, it can take you totally off track. Sure enough, I found that "feature creep" lives in the offline world too.

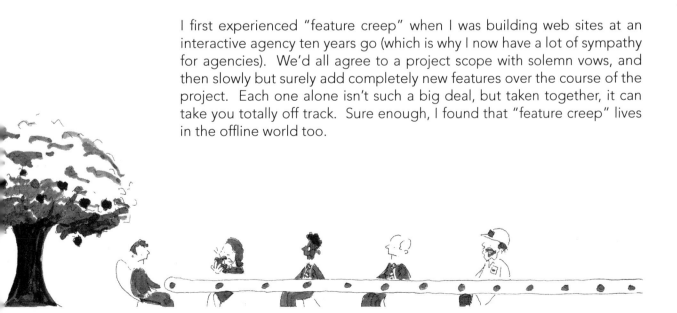

Tom Fishburne

January 3, 2006

I'm amazed how often I hear of buzz marketing as it it's just another tactical marketing program, like an FSI or a direct mail campaign. The nature of "buzz" is that you're not in control of what's getting "buzzed" about. Your best hope is to start with a remarkable product or service that is "buzz-worthy" and then get it in the right people's hands.

January 30, 2006

I sketched this one just after interviewing with method, the challenger brand I ended up joining the following month. I snuck their iconic bowling pin-shaped dish wash bottle in the far right. I hadn't accepted the job yet, but it was my little inside joke. Brand Camp sometimes feels like a diary and I often hide little personal cues inside the cartoons.

Tom Fishburne

February 12, 2006

I drew this cartoon after a withering executive product council meeting. They even set the room that day as if it was the UN, with a ring of executives around a table with a microphone. One by one, we were trooped in to present our stage gate briefs and subject ourselves to questioning. Around this time, someone described one of the winning product ideas as a peace treaty, and it struck me how many ideas are compromised by having to compromise.

February 26, 2006

Every brand has yearly margin improvement targets to hit and usually a price increase is off the table. Material costs seem to be increasing all the time, so what's a brand manager to do? Usually number four (which I think is one of the reasons private label is gaining so much traction). Otherwise, you have to get creative. I've seen each and every one of these in practice.

My hat's off to Dannon yogurt for simply taking out product and claiming that there was "now room for your favorite mix-ins". Clever.

Tom Fishburne

March 14, 2006

This cartoon was inspired by Doug Hall, author of "Jump Start Your Brain" and founder of Eureka Ranch. He writes about the art of the brainstorm, and criticizes the typical corporate approach that he dubs "braindraining". A year later, I met Doug in person when we spoke at the same conference and gave him this cartoon, along with a few others. I was really excited when he then decided to use a bunch of my cartoons to illustrate an Innovation Manifesto he wrote.

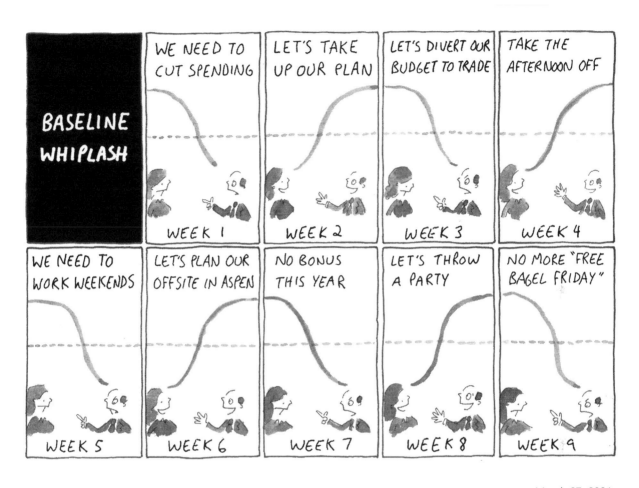

March 27, 2006

I'm convinced that looking at Nielsen sales data week by week will give you an ulcer or drive you insane. There are constant ups and downs. It's really the long-term trend that matters. But, I've worked on a number of brands that religiously monitored baseline performance week by week (one boss called these "worm races"). When sales dipped down one week, a black cloud hovered in the office. When sales were up the next, the sun was shining. This was made off the more frustrating that it's very hard to impact baseline volume in the short-term (unlike promotional volume), so there's not a lot you can do (except spend a lot of time scenario-planning).

Tom Fishburne

April 10, 2006

I often get cartoon ideas in the middle of meetings, and it's a real challenge to look serious and interested in the conversation while I'm scribbling madly in the margins. This cartoon was inspired in a meeting to unveil a new "decision matrix". After I published this cartoon, I feigned a little ignorance and said that it was inspired by a previous job. Works every time.

April 17, 2006

I once heard that every company is either a rule maker, a rule breaker, or a rule follower. I drew this cartoon after seeing a Goliath consumer packaged good company come out with a product eerily close to one of ours. This cartoon then found its way into our company handbook.

Tom Fishburne

May 1, 2006

This cartoon was inspired by one of my old business school professors, Stephan Thomke, who taught us all about development funnels. Every company has some form of this, where you start with wide set of options and gradually narrow to a few. However, far too often, the opposite can happen.

May 15, 2006

I came from an agency background before marketing, so I know there's disfunctional behavior on both sides of the table (and I like making fun of both). But agency selective hearing is a particular problem. It reminded me of the classic Far Side cartoon on what dogs hear.

I thought the cartoon was funny, but it prompted some peeved emails from some of the account directors I've worked with in the past.

And an avalanche of support from my coworkers.

Tom Fishburne

May 29, 2006

Polarizing is a dirty word in concept development. But, I think it's generally better to be selectively loved than universally liked. Particularly in the sea of undifferentiated products struggling to compete with private label. As my friend Eric likes to say, "there are riches in the niches".

June 12, 2006

I've seen this happen time and time again. A group comes up with a truly unique idea, and over the course of development, the unique bits get sanded off and polished, and the resulting product is a pale shadow of the original idea.

Many companies become a factory for "safe" ideas. What if, instead of scissors and shears, each step in development boosted the idea and make it more and more remarkable, rather than safer and safer?

Tom Fishburne

June 26, 2006

You always hear that managing a brand is like being the CEO of your own small business. You get your very own P&L.

But, it's always an eye-opener when you first inherit a P&L and discover how little you can actually impact in the short term. Most traditional marketing tactics steer the brand in the long term. When you're off plan, the first thing to do is cut marketing spend.

July 10, 2006

This cartoon was inspired by an executive who was notorious for bringing home sales samples to his wife for her feedback. You'd then get a random piece of feedback from out of nowhere. Usually right before launch. Often with no real understanding at all of what you were trying to accomplish with the launch.

Tom Fishburne

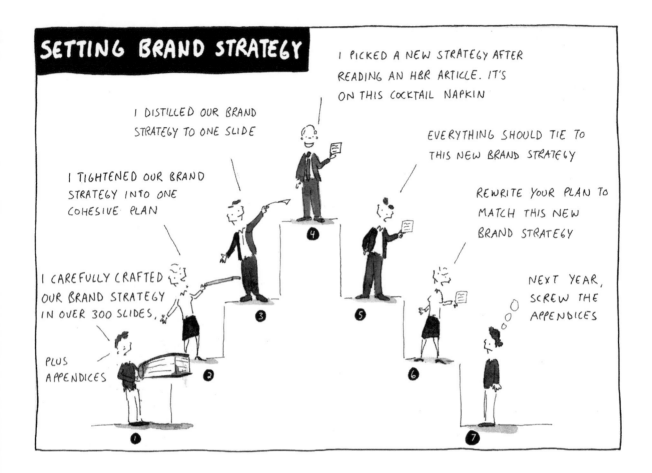

August 11, 2006

The planning process is such a funny ritual, particularly in large organization. A bottoms-up plan bubbles up and a top-down plan trickles down.

When you're starting out, pitching plan is basically career day. It may be your only time to shine in front of the leadership team. So you work nights and weekends to create a weighty tome, complete with appendices.

It's always a little depressing when your plan gets boiled down in the next round to one page, and then six months later, you're in a totally different place anyway and wonder why you put all that work into it.

54

September 4, 2006

This cartoon was inspired by working on a challenger brand and reading lots of Adam Morgan, including his challenger brand manifesto, "Eat Big Fish". When you're out-matched on resources and sheer size, you have to keep changing the rules in order to survive.

Tom Fishburne

September 11, 2006

I once worked in a really depressing office floor just before it was refurbished. It had high cubicle walls, a ceiling about a foot over our heads, no natural light, and really bad halogen lights.

The ironic footnote is that our brand positioning centered on health and wellness.

September 25, 2006

I love working on brand architectures and positioning statements. It's fun to wordsmith and psychoanalyze. But, some of the language cracks me up. And you know that the actual consumers you write about would never acknowledge the actual insights literally.

Tom Fishburne

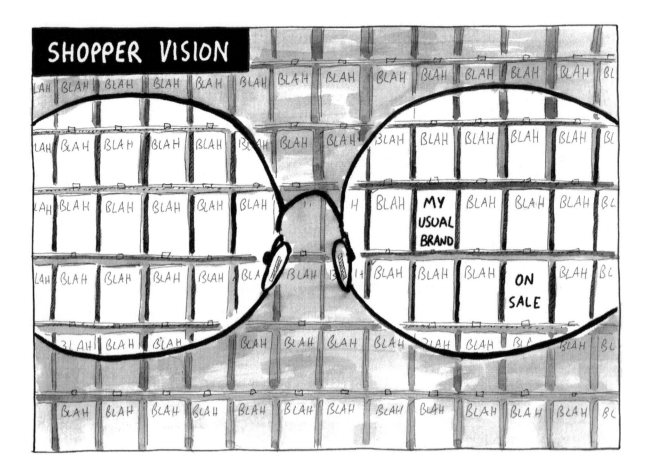

October 2, 2006

The average consumer spends just 3-5 seconds at the shelf. Which is funny when you think about how much time you spend on the subtle nuances of packaging design.

October 9, 2006

I'm addicted to Law & Order, particularly the ones with Lenny Briscoe. This cartoon was inspired after a day of focus groups moderated by someone from the ad agency. She obviously liked one concept more than the others, and was asking a lot of leading questions. It made me think how easily the moderator can sway the outcome.

Tom Fishburne

October 16, 2006

At method, we often repeat the motto that "safe is risky." It made me think about which ideas typically survive in companies. It's usually the safest ones.

This cartoon works a lot better in color. There is one psychedelic butterfly fluttering in a monotonous sky of grey ones.

This cartoon is the inverse of Seth Godin's "Purple Cow", where truly remarkable ideas, the purple cows, are what are remembered and shared by consumers.

So, why do companies so often chase the opposite?

November 6, 2006

This is one of those autobiographical cartoons. Writing anything in a group is tough, but particularly a two word brand promise that the entire brand team needs to support. I actually spent 6 months of grammatical infighting with a team only to come up with "healthy haven". Which sounded good to us, if only to make the process stop.

And then, our director didn't like the word, "haven".

Tom Fishburne

November 13, 2006

Forgive me, oh creative gods, for I have been each and every one of these (particularly the "Wannabe").

Apparently, a lot of others have as well, because this cartoon really made the blog rounds.

A creative director in New Zealand even requested a high-resolution version to frame and hang in his office as a precaution to clients.

November 27, 2006

I drew this cartoon while feeling fatique at green as a status symbol. I went to a cocktail party and heard a lot of green one-up-manship.

Tom Fishburne

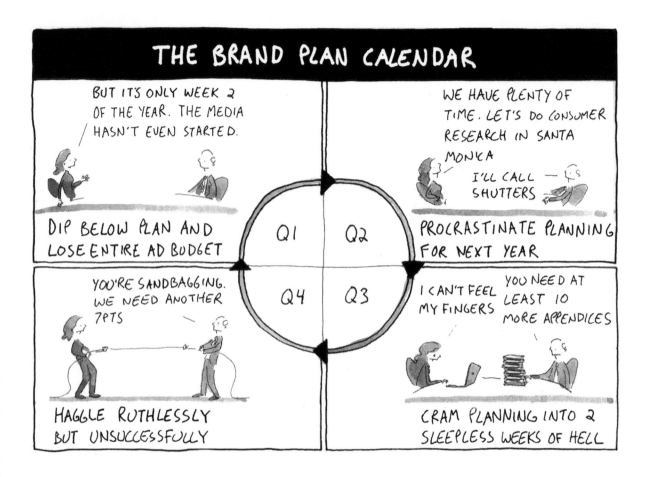

December 4, 2006

I thought it would be fun to parody each quarter of a brand planning year. After such methodical and grueling planning, it always amazes me how the marketing budget can be cut unceremonially just a few weeks into the new year.

Everytime I hear of a marketing junket to Los Angeles, whether for research or an ad shoot, the hotel Shutters (right on the beach in Santa Monica) always seems to be part of the plan.

December 11, 2006

This cartoon was inspired by a package design review. I had spent a lot of time crafting a creative brief and was struck by all of the marketing terminology, which would be lost on most consumers. We then tested the packaging with consumers, and they missed a few of the key takeaways.

It cracked me up to think about cutting to the chase and just including the actual creative brief.

Tom Fishburne

December 18, 2006

This cartoon came after a particularly brutal bout with PowerPoint. No surprise they are known as "pitches". It sometimes feels like we invest more work in continually selling our ideas than in actually creating anything. It cracked me up to think of that selling process as a supply chain as methodical as the actual supply chain for our products.

January 8, 2007

Most clients ask for really breakthrough creative from their agencies, but few actually run with it. They often take the safe route. If they take the safe route long enough, the agency just stops serving up the risky fare after a while. This cartoon was inspired by something I read from Adam Morgan.

Tom Fishburne

January 15, 2007

It really is a little scary how few new products actually survive the first year. I had seen this 25% figure in a report, but it's a lot lower if you look over two to three years. Yet, there's an absolute explosion in the sheer number of new products that launch every year, which I think helps drive the churn even more.

January 22, 2007

This cartoon is in the same vein as the previous cartoon, but came out of the play on words in the title. Once I had the name, it made me think of new product development process as throwing spaghetti against the wall to see what sticks.

Tom Fishburne

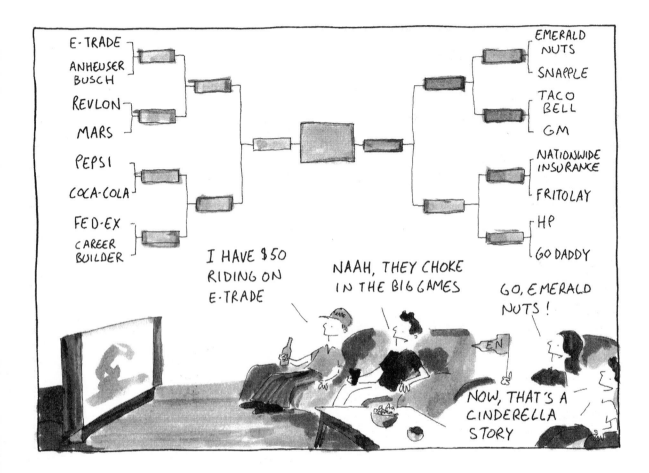

February 5, 2007

I think that watching the Superbowl for the advertising is a universal marketing trait. This drives my football-obsessed brother crazy.

We used to hold marketing interviews right after the annual Superbowl, and our favorite question was to have them analyze their favorite Superbowl ad.

On a related note, Emerald Nuts really is a Cinderella story. I once met their marketing team at an award ceremony. They're a nut producer from the middle of nowhere with no history of advertising that suddenly decided to build a brand on the back of a very quirky and memorable ad campaign with Goodby Silverstein.

February 12, 2007

This cartoon was inspired by a first meeting with a new advertising and interactive agency. We held the meeting in their largest conference room and they seriously outnumbered us, with people sitting around the whole perimeter who didn't talk in the whole meeting. I think they were trying to impress us with the extent of their resources, but all I could think of was the overhead. The next several conference calls were all impossible to schedule because they involved specialists who worked on so many other projects.

Tom Fishburne

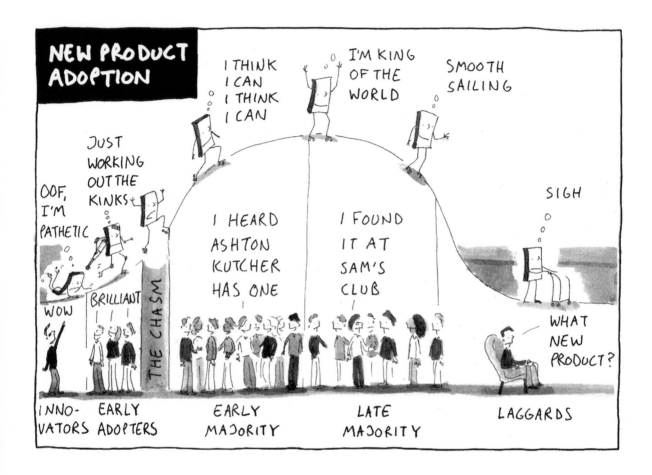

February 26, 2007

I found myself referring to Geoffrey Moore's "Crossing the Chasm" model so often, I eventually needed to create a cartoon on it. Moore originally created the model to talk about the adoption of technology products, but I find that it works really well with the adoption of any sort of marketing trend.

March 5, 2007

I read an article on the explosion of greenwashing, and the author joked that next we'd see Captain Crunch unveiling a "save the manatees" program.

Nothing against the Captain, the Leprechaun, the Dough Boy, or any of these particular equity characters though. I just picked them because they helped personalize the idea, and because they stand for traditional advertising. It amazed me how many emails I got from people who worked on these particular brands and took some offence. Sorry, Captain.

Tom Fishburne

March 19, 2007

I drew this cartoon while moving from the US to the UK, so I felt a bit like a marketer without borders. I was wondering what would be similar and what would be different. Anyway, I took the idea to the extreme and this cartoon popped out.

THE
LAST
MILE

WE LOVE THE AD
BUT WE CAN'T SEE
OUR BRANDING

YOUR LOGO IS IN
THE CORNER

THAT SPECK?!? ARE
YOU KIDDING?

OK, WE'VE NOW
INCREASED IT BY
0.005%

WE NEED IT AT
LEAST 50% LARGER.
CAN WE SEE A RANGE?

HERE IT IS AT 1% LARGER,
BUT THIS COMPROMISES
OUR ARTISTIC INTEGRITY

MY BOSS IS CALLING
YOUR BOSS

FINE! HERE'S 50,000%
LARGER... BUT WE'VE NOW
MISSED THE PRINT DEADLINE

March 26, 2007

This cartoon had been marinating for about a year and a half after an experience that pretty much followed this script. "Make the logo bigger" is an eternal debate. Every client wants their logo bigger and every agency thinks it jeopardizes the creative. It usually leads to a pretty tense tug-o-war. Can't we all just get along?

My old manager Gulbin emailed me in stitches after reading this cartoon because she knew exactly its inspiration.

Tom Fishburne

May 14, 2007

This cartoon was inspired by my visit to a trade show in London, filled with literally thousands of brands touting the next superfood or wonder eco ingredient. The funniest was something called Poo Poo paper, stationary made from elephant droppings. It reminded me of another high-priced product I'd seen in London called Weasel coffee, which comes from a coffee bean literally eaten, digested, and dropped by weasels. What a marketing achievement to literally make excrement this valuable.

I drew this cartoon after meeting with lots of marketing agencies in London and learning that we didn't have nearly enough budget to break through the clutter. It also made me think how much media terminology is taken from the military, as if you're going to overwhelm your consumers with "shock and awe".

Tom Fishburne

June 11, 2007

Brand onions, brand architectures, brand pyramids. There are infinite devices to write your positioning statment. It can be a thought-provoking exercise. But, far too often, people take them way too seriously. The danger is getting to a point where you never question it, as if it's written in stone.

June 18, 2007

I had a truly awful customer service experience with a company called Vonage. That same day, I received an expensive glossy direct marketing piece from them in the mail. It made me think how epidemic bad customer service is in general.

When you think about how much money and effort is spent on finding and reaching consumers, it seems crazy to throw it all away by not respecting them enough to provide good customer service. The least paid people in a company are usually those who answer the consumer phone. Yet, they are the ones who can have the biggest impact on how a consumer feels about a brand.

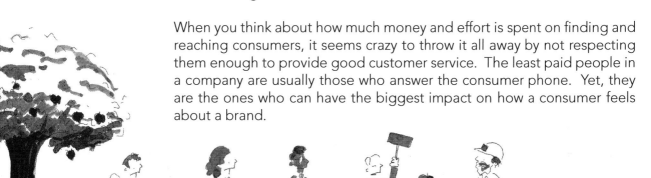

Tom Fishburne

June 26, 2008

The inspiration for this week's cartoon came via an email from Satyam Viswanathan, who works in brand management in India. I just love getting emails like his from other parts of the world. It goes to show that dysfunctional marketing shenanigans are universal.

July 2, 2007

This cartoon idea sprang fully formed from a New York Times piece on the ridiculous lengths that some brands were going to be considered for the Home Depot Eco Options promotion (including, yes, a brand of electric chainsaw). The issue is not as white and black as the old treehugger/lumberjack dynamic.

Tom Fishburne

July 9, 2007

So many brand cross-promotions wind up feeling a bit shallow and opportunistic to me (embarassingly including a few from my past). Plus, there's always that funny, slightly awkward conversation when two brand managers first feel each other out to do a promotion. It got me thinking of it all as a kind of singles bar.

CONSUMERS ARE LOOKING FOR "AUTHENTICITY" NOWADAYS. BRANDS WITH A BACKSTORY. ARTISAN-MADE NOT MASS-PRODUCED. NATURAL NOT ARTIFICIAL. ETHICS NOT PROFITS.

SO WHAT "AUTHENTIC BACKSTORY" CAN WE COOK UP FOR YOU, MARSHMALLOW MAN? THINK BIG, WHAT WILL GET YOU INTO WHOLEFOODS?

WELL, THE LAB THAT MAKES MY TETRASODIUM PYROPHOSPHATE HAS A PENSION

TOM FISHBURNE

July 16, 2007

I read a quote somewhere that "authenticity cannot be cooked up after the fact". It struck me at a natural products show how many up-and-coming brands are peddling "authenticity" as their key brand asset. I then strolled a typical supermarket, and saw many of the big, mass-market brands trying to do the same thing (particularly in relation to the environment), even if the actual nature and history of the brands didn't really support that.

Also, I always loved that Ghostbuster scene with the Stay Puft Marshmallow Man. I later learned that character was inspired by the Pillsbury Dough Boy and the Michelin Man. Gotta love equity characters.

Tom Fishburne

July 20, 2007

I drew a few custom cartoons for a conference on sensory science. As someone who used to get in trouble for drawing cartoons during science class, it gave me great pleasure to be invited to contribute to a whole science conference. Anyway, here's one of those cartoons not part of my regular series.

Can you imagine being on the brand team of WOW potato chips when the FDA introduced this mandatory warning label in 1998 on olestra, your secret ingredient? Wow is right.

July 23, 2007

I first saw this behavior a few years ago, and some of us referred to it as the "[Product X] hangover". An ambitious new product launch had tanked (as those pesky new products will often do), and many of the people who had worked on it had been fired. It left a tangible level of fear and risk-aversion for years. "We don't want another 'X'". "We tried that before and look what happened." And on an on. No amount of "innovation workshops" could shake it.

How rare it is for a CEO at the yearly company offsite to celebrate the "failures" and the lessons learned from them? How inspiring it would be if he or she did?

Tom Fishburne

July 30, 2007

This cartoon idea came mostly from the play on words in the title. It just cracked me up to think of someone having a crisis with their brand identity. Marketers tend to write brand positioning statements as if the brand was the single most important thing in the consumer's life.

August 13, 2007

This cartoon was inspired by the perfectionist zeal marketers have for aspects of our brand that most consumers never notice, particularly minor packaging details. I once spent a whole afternoon at a photoshoot of black raspberries debating whether or not to Photoshop out the little hairs on the raspberries. I never knew that raspberries were so hairy, but they really are (particularly enlarged on a monitor). I sure felt silly telling my wife how I spent my day, and she reminded me that consumers would never know one way or another.

It got me thinking what a dream it would be if people really noticed and appreciated all of the crazy lengths we go.

Tom Fishburne

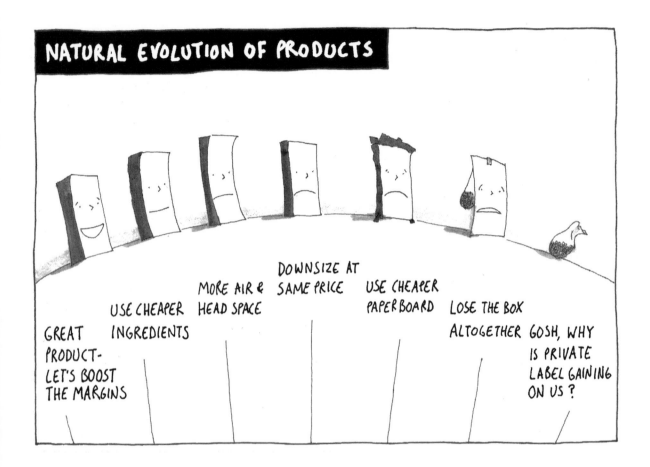

August 27, 2007

I took my four year old daughter to the Natural History Museum and we had an entertaining chat about evolution. It got me thinking about branded products, and how most product evolutions have to do with margin improvement rather than better performance. Consumers may not notice one round of cost-cuts, but over time, the reduced product quality can become obvious. Why is it that cereal boxes never close properly after you open them once? My guess is that little "advance" caused a 0.4 point margin gain at some point in the 90's. But, oh how irritating to consumers.

Of course, continuous margin improvement taken to an extreme gets hit by Darwinism too. Not from a pack of hyena, but from a pack of private label - which actually seems to be getting better over time.

September 17, 2007

I have to remind myself sometimes that my brand is not the most important thing in a target consumer's life. I think a lot of brand positioning statements are written as if the consumers are constantly thinking and obsessing about the brand. When I hear the description, "brand loyalist", I envision a groupie with a logo tattooed on her forehead.

Obviously, even "brand loyalists" have complex lives completely separate from our brands. As marketers, I think it's good to remember the actual role that we play in consumers' very human lives, and not overstep the significance of a brand of, say, "pickle relish".

Tom Fishburne

September 24, 2007

I find many eco labels incredibly confusing (and I'm probably a lot closer to them than the average consumer). Because there are few regulatory standards, there seem to be a lot of "eco labels of the week". Even the standard ones are confusing, as you can see when the Vegan Society withdrew its certification from Ecover, because they consider "no animal testing" to include a variety of 0.2mm long water flea.

It got me thinking that in our rush to communicate eco-friendly benefits, we're building our own Tower of Eco Babel. Thanks to Wikipedia, I learned the root of Babel means to "confuse or confound" in Hebrew.

October 8, 2007

This cartoon was prompted by the expression, "you can't cut your way to top-line growth". More companies seem to be equipped with "cutting tools" than "growing tools". Also, the typical Stage Gate process is better designed for trimming rather than for boosting ideas. I also think that companies often put all of their hopes in one or two new products, and then leave the rest of their pipeline pretty dry, rather than have lots of sapling ideas at various stages of growth. That can be a problem when those few "hero" ideas get watered down beyond all recognition and then are launched anyway because there's nothing else there.

Tom Fishburne

October 15, 2007

I came across an article in Ad Age about companies getting caught by consumers committing "green murder". It talked about marketers putting out "green briefs" to agencies to find something worth talking about their environmental impacts without actually changing anything. In this rush to reposition everyday brands as environmentally-friendly, there seems to be collective amnesia of the inconsistencies in the story. And by being so vocal (particularly as a johnny-come-lately), these brands are actually quite naked and exposed. It's only a matter of time before a consumer calls out, "but he has nothing on."

Since there are no perfectly sustainable businesses, we're all a bit naked and exposed on this. I think the only way is come across with honesty and humility and an open recognition that it's about progress, not perfection.

January 24, 2005

I've grumbled about Stage Gate my whole brand career. So, I was excited to meet "Jumpstart your Brain" author Doug Hall at an event where he skewered the entire Stage Gate process as "Corporate Communism".

He emailed me a week later that "the talk in London got me on a roll - so I decided to really take a big shot at Corporate Communism. Any chance I can motivate you to do a cartoon about how the Central Command oppresses the little guy?" He included this cartoon in an article for the American Creativity Association journal called "The Rise of Corporate Communism and the Fall of American Innovation".

Tom Fishburne

October 29, 2007

Thanks to my friend Clint for sharing the term "focus group diva". As Clint explained it:

"I earned my 'focus group' diva nickname by having our lunch delivered to the facility from an hour away. The group was in Detroit, and there is a great deli in Ann Arbor that I visit every time I'm in Michigan (it's called Zingerman's and the sandwiches rock). The facility offered the menu and I picked it. To the untrained eyes of my co-workers, ordering sandwiches from an hour away seemed kind of silly (they came around on the sandwiches)."

It's funny, the back room of a focus group is really kind of like the marketer's "green room". Only without smashing the monitor Keith Moon-style.

November 5, 2007

I haven't worked in a public company for a while, but I definitely remember that fish bowl feeling. I was emailing with someone recently about public CPG companies, and the growing sense that innovation is just as important to Wall street as it is to consumers. "Street cred" was used to describe the intent of more and more new products initiatives. I found this concept very funny.

And it's always nice to have a reason to use the expression, "for shizzle".

Tom Fishburne

November 12, 2007

I gave a little talk to a group of marketers at Pepsi. When they originally asked me to speak, we talked about one of the dilemmas of innovation in a large company. Senior management want to be included in the decisions, but they don't have enough time to really be in the loop. By the time they have a moment to swoop in, the team has already moved on. This often leads to "decisions" being "re-decided". Mulling this over, the Sisyphus metaphor popped to mind.

November 19, 2007

I heard a talk on the challenge of creating new products in companies with deeply separate functional silos. It can take a peace treaty to get a product through this system, so the "safest" products win.

Too often, I think, it ends up like this cartoon, with too many puppeteers at odds. And the consumer gets the same old, same old.

Of course, the best products are strongest because of the diverse teams that work on them. I think Apple is one of the best at this: bringing together structural design, interface design, licensing, and more in a coordinated way.

Tom Fishburne

December 3, 2007

Obviously, not all retail partnerships work like this. But, I do feel like the typical starting point can be pretty adversarial.

I was chatting with a trade director at a large retailer and he explained how they tier the meeting rooms. "The little ones by the lobby are for people we don't like, the ones in the main floor are for people we like OK, and we never, ever bring suppliers up to our floor. I don't want them to even guess what I think." Luckily, we weren't meeting in the lobby when he told me this.

I've been fortunate to work with many buyers who think about partnerships in the true sense. But, so many retailers seem to look at brands purely on a transactional basis, I think they can miss the bigger opportunity.

December 10, 2007

This cartoon was inspired after a conversation with the head of sustainability for a British retailer. He said he was conflicted about carbon labeling. There's a big push here to add a numeric carbon footprint to all consumer products. It seems like a good disclosure in spirit, and the sheer effort to measure the carbon footprint is a good thing, which leads to ideas on how to reduce that footprint.

But, labeling on packaging is a complicated one for consumers. For one thing, it's confusing. Do consumers really understand what a 75g carbon label on a bag of crisps means? For another thing, it can create mixed messages like the one in this cartoon.

Tom Fishburne

December 17, 2007

I always found the island of misfit toys from the Rudolph movie a bit creepy. Each toy sings a few lines about why they are misfits and that they were abandoned because kids didn't want them.

My mind wandered watching it with the kids and it dawned on me that these toys are actually just outputs of product development gone awry. A lot of product launches wind up as misfits. So, it made me chuckle to think of these toys articulating the reasons that made them misfits. I guess the typical new product development process is just as dysfunctional for elves.

January 7, 2008

'Tis the season in early January to make resolutions. Including many that fall quickly by the wayside. It's only human of course. That's why gym memberships try to lock you into a long contract.

Something about the idea of brands/products making resolutions just like the rest of us cracks me up. Particularly since marketing is full of same foibles that we all share.

Tom Fishburne

January 14, 2008

I was at a farmer's market and started wondering what it would be like if everyone had to put their brand or product on display in a "market" like this. Then, my mind jumped from "farmer" to "pharma" and out popped this cartoon.

I find the explosion in direct-to-consumer drug ads fascinating and more than a little creepy (particularly the embarrassing side effects). I learned that the US is the only industrialized country in the world that allows them.

The idea of a "pharmer's market" felt like a pretty good metaphor for the shopper-oriented drug marketplace in the US.

January 28, 2008

I jotted the pencil sketch of this cartoon on a plane returning from a bunch of meetings like this. I started thinking about how convoluted decision-making can be. There's that old saying that a failure to decide is still a decision.

It cracks me up whenever I hear, "let's take this decision offline", in a meeting because the subtext feels like a welcome delay tactic. Everyone's relieved to just keep the meeting moving.

Tom Fishburne

February 4, 2008

I was thinking how communication gets a little squirrelly inside companies. Something gets interpreted out of context and then passed along down the line just like that telephone game we all played in kindergarten.

I think this gets even worse with geographical distance. I worked at a company once with the R&D center a full five-hour drive from where all the brand managers sat. Things used to fester all the time. The only way to keep communication smooth was to meet face-to-face as often as possible. We sometimes used to hop in the car, drive five hours for a two-hour meeting and then five hours back in a day. But it was worth it.

February 11, 2008

I drew this cartoon thinking about some of the debates I've seen about squeezing just one more product benefit on the front of a package. Insisting on too many benefits front-and-center cuts back the impact of any one. It's often hard to agree to the lead benefit, so products become the result of a peace treaty. Also, many benefits have become so commonplace, they lose their meaning entirely.

All of that clutter made me think of it as attribute soup, which reminded me of that old "too many cooks spoil the broth" quote.

Tom Fishburne

February 18, 2008

This cartoon was inspired by a meeting with sustainability activist Michael Braungart (who co-wrote the thought-provoking book "Cradle to Cradle"). He helped expand our thinking about eco responsibility to being less about one attribute or another, and more about a holistic approach of thinking through the past, present, and future of every product.

The next time I trolled the supermarket, I was really struck by some of the confusing eco claim one-up-manship. So many products were suddenly trumpeting one eco claim or another, and much of it seemed ridiculous, confusing, or disingenuous.

THE 8 TYPES OF CREATIVE DIRECTORS

THE ARTIST — "THIS FSI SHALL BE MY OPUS"

THE DIVA — "THERE'S NOT ENOUGH GENUFLECTING IN THIS BRIEF"

THE GENIUS — "I CAME UP WITH THE WHOLE CAMPAIGN ON THE SUBWAY THIS MORNING"

THE MESSIAH — "MY VISION FOR THE BRAND IS DIVINE AND UNQUESTIONABLE"

THE OVERBOOKED

THE DRAMA QUEEN — "I JUST CAN'T WORK UNDER THESE CONDITIONS... LIKE DEADLINES"

THE SENSITIVE TYPE — "CRITICIZING MY WORK IS LIKE CRITICIZING MY CHILDREN"

THE ART NAZI — "NO REVISIONS FOR YOU!"

February 25, 2008

I've been really fortunate to have worked mostly with Creative Directors in "The Genius" camp (at least, I have to say that or I might get blackballed). But, I couldn't resist poking a little fun at some of the other archetypes. And obviously there's a little bit of each type within everyone.

Tom Fishburne

March 3, 2008

I was thinking how many package promotions seem gratuitous.

I actually love the idea of a "Free Prize Inside", and found Seth Godin's book by that name really inspiring. But I think that often the "free prize" just doesn't connect as well to the product as it could. It could be any prize and any product.

I remember someone at General Mills comparing two promotions that had run with Cheerios. In one, they gave away $5 off of a Dominos Pizza. And, in another, they gave away a free children's book that mothers could read with their kids. Given that the Cheerios brand promise was "nurturing", it's pretty clear why one was the better and more memorable fit.

March 10, 2008

An old colleague emailed me to ask if I'd ever done a cartoon on product naming. She was helping a friend start a naming company.

I was surprised to discover that I'd never covered product naming. I have certainly been in lots and lots of ridiculous naming sessions over the years, but for some reason had never turned those into a cartoon.

So, Janine, this one's for you.

Tom Fishburne

March 31, 2008

I like ideations as much as the next guy. Particularly when there are good snacks. I just think they are too often treated as a cure-all. Need an innovation? Just hold an ideation. I don't think that an isolated brainstorm once a year is the best approach for coming up with innovations. I think it works better when innovation is a constant, continuous process involving everyone.

There's also this funny "find your inner hippy" dynamic that often happens in setting up an ideation. It often feels that if you set the right mood (room, props, music, snacks, etc.), the ideas will just come. This environment can feel superficial, because when you leave the room the dynamic is so different. In the cold light of the office, it's easier and more acceptable to criticize and squash ideas, rather than find creative ways to grow them.

April 7, 2008

I always struggle with giving creative feedback. I can only imagine what's it's like to be a creative director and have your work (which is inherently personal) continually critiqued in front of you. I guess you learn to grow really thick skin (or plug your ears discretely).

So, I always try to dose my creative feedback to others with plenty of ego stroking. An early manager of mine described it as a "criticism sandwich", which led to this cartoon.

Tom Fishburne

April 14, 2008

I once worked in an Internet startup that grew from 25 employees to 2,500 in 3 years. In the midst of it all, I first started thinking about "the process pendulum". Our process swung erratically from nonexistent to command-and-control. We were scrappy and entrepreneurial in year one, and then we added layer after layer of bureaucracy to restrain the chaos of so much growth.

I've always liked that Steve Jobs' quote, "it's more fun to be a pirate than to join the navy". But what do you do when the pirate ship grows to the size and complexity of a navy ship? How do you keep small even as you grow big?

This cartoon was inspired by Seth Godin's book, Meatball Sundae. He writes about the rush of companies jumping on the "new marketing" bandwagon. Some companies are leaping into myspace, youtube, and blogging in exactly the same self-serving way they approach TV advertising – by trying to "interrupt" consumers from what they were doing. This obviously misses the point. Consumers are gravitating to "new marketing" channels exactly because they are in control, not the brands. And certain brands are mismatched completely with new marketing ... just like, say, meatballs and sundaes.

Tom Fishburne

April 28, 2008

I heard someone described as a "control freak", and it struck me that there was actually another type, the "out-of-control-freak". A senior manager who assumes total control of a project or area, but actually doesn't have the time or interest to really understand it.

It made me think of this funny dynamic that happens when a project becomes either a raging success or a dismal failure. People seem to climb out of the woodwork to claim partial credit for a successful project. Yet a failed project is often pinned to a few scapegoats.

May 5, 2008

I came across an article on the environmental ills of outdoor media: lots of paper, lots of fuel to drive to media sites, toxic glues, etc. The next time I rode the Tube, I was struck by how many outdoor ads were touting some environmental benefit. I put the two together and it felt very ironic.

The trouble with much of the environmental grand-standing right now is that it tends to focus on one attribute or another, not a holistic approach of making a company more sustainable over time. So, there's often more than a bit of hypocrisy if you look hard enough. The same company that garnered a packaging reduction is printing out masses of paper to tell the world about it, which kind of defeats the purpose.

Tom Fishburne

May 12, 2008

This cartoon was inspired by John Grant's "Green Marketing Manifesto", a thought-provoking book on how marketers like us should approach the green marketplace.

"You can't just decide 'ethical is in' and treat it like a fashion." I read this line in John's book and it prompted this cartoon idea. It's been interesting to watch so many companies trot out their Corporate and Social Responsibility plans recently.

This is great when it's serious, but a problem when it's superficial and publicity-driven. Because consumers can see right through it.

May 19, 2008

I went to a marketing sustainability steering committee meeting, and someone in the group was talking about company transparency, and how reluctant many companies are to reveal their inner workings. The traditional approach is to concoct a persona via advertising and point to that instead.

Yet, more and more consumers seem to be looking for the company behind the curtain. They're no longer as swayed by the concocted brand image of advertising. Instead, consumers want to know who's behind the products they buy.

Tom Fishburne

May 24, 2008

On every brand team I've joined, we've spent some time "climbing the benefit ladder" from product benefits to emotional benefits, trying to mine some emotional insight that will cause consumers to give our brand their undying loyalty.

I've always enjoyed these sessions, but also find them really funny. It's just so rare in the business workplace to talk about emotional issues at all. There's something ridiculous about sitting around a corporate conference table talking about the guilt experienced by a time-stressed mother of three. And why this guilt can only be sated by our brand of frozen broccoli-with-cheese-sauce. Or tile grout.

THE FIVE STAGES OF MISSING PLAN

I'M CONFIDENT WE'LL MAKE IT ALL UP BY Q4	WHO CAME UP WITH THIS CRAZY PLAN ANYWAY?	WE'D BE ON PLAN IF IT WEREN'T FOR THE WEATHER, THE ECONOMY, THE ELECTION, THE...	WHAT WILL THIS DO TO MY BONUS?	I ACCEPT THAT THIS PLAN WAS TOTALLY UNREALISTIC AND CREATED BY SADISTS
DENIAL	**ANGER**	**BARGAINING**	**DEPRESSION**	**ACCEPTANCE**

June 2, 2008

I was thinking of the funny dance we all do in "meeting plan" (hitting your volume targets). Whenever you're off, the easiest thing to do is blame the plan itself and whoever committed to it in the first place (which is particularly funny when it was you).

There's a lot of nuance around timing and when and how to communicate that you're off plan. The process reminded me of Kübler-Ross' "Five Stages of Grief".

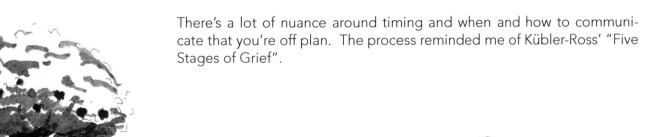

Tom Fishburne

June 9, 2008

I love going to factories. Putting on the hard hat and lab coat and seeing where the magic happens. It makes me feel like Willy Wonka. Massive humming machines. Thousands of containers whizzing by on conveyer belts.

But, the inner workings of a plant always seem like a stark contrast from the persona put across on the label. Particularly if the brand has any kind of provenance. The "family recipe" doesn't seem so homey when it's being blended by a guy wearing a beard net.

June 16, 2008

I took my family camping on a goat's milk farm and asked the farmer what he thought about organic farming. He said that organic foods were a "rich man's luxury".

It got me thinking about the impact of a recession on ethical consumerism. As consumer's start squeezing their pocketbooks, how will this affect brands with a social mission that also carry a premium?

Tom Fishburne

June 24, 2008

I think that cause marketing, when done right, can be extremely positive. When I worked on Yoplait, I saw first-hand how powerful their "save lids to save lives" campaign with the Susan G. foundation was in raising awareness and creating donations.

But I've been feeling a little cause marketing fatigue. I like corporate philanthropy and I think it's great that more and more companies and brands are embracing cause marketing. I think that business can be a real agent of change. But, it's easy to come across as flippant, disingenuous, or gratuitous.

And there seems to be quite a bit of "causewashing" at the moment.

June 30, 2008

I picked up a book recently called Shades of Green, which has a spectrum of eco tips for people based on how green they consider themselves, from dark green to light green.

It made me think about the different motivations for people thinking green and I thought it would be fun to play with a few stereotypes.

Tom Fishburne

July 7, 2008

There's something called the bullwhip effect in supply chains, where one action magnifies exponentially downstream, like the cracking of a bull-whip.

I've been thinking there is a bullwhip effect within organizations too. No one likes change, but of course it's constant in business. But, when change happens, I've noticed the ripple effect is often harder than the change it-self. Particularly in the immediate chaotic aftermath when everything is up for grabs and people are trying to figure out which way is up.

WHEN THE ECONOMY THROWS YOU EGGS, MAKE 'EM SCRAMBLED

THIS IS YOUR BRAND

THIS IS YOUR BRAND IN A RECESSION

THIS IS YOUR BRAND IN A RECESSION WITH A LITTLE CREATIVITY, A DASH OF OPPORTUNISM, AND SOME PATIENCE

July 14, 2008

It's obviously true that consumers change behavior during a recession. But, I think there's a big opportunity for brands to adapt to provide a new story.

I think the key is to keep your cool, avoid the temptation to drastically cut budgets, and take a fresh look at your brand in the light of the recession. Rethink the role your brand can plan for your consumers now.

Because I do think there's room to be optimistic. Even with recession news on the doorstep.

about me

I draw cartoons and work in marketing. In 2002, I started lampooning business in a marketing cartoon called Brand Camp about life on the M&M bowl side of the focus group glass.

I learned to draw cartoons on the backs of Harvard Business School cases while a student there. I started Brand Camp a few years later by tacking the cartoons to the side of my cubicle at General Mills and emailing them to a handful of friends. I soon started getting emails from people in companies all over the world.

Brand Camp has grown by word of mouth to reach thousands of marketers each week and appears regularly in blogs, web sites, and publications such as Brandweek, Market Leader, and the Asian Wall Street Journal. I also do quite a bit of speaking at campuses, conferences, and companies with my cartoons.

When not cartooning, I'm Senior Marketing Director of Europe for method, a challenger brand that is trying to exploit a lot of the stuff I lampoon in my cartoons. I previously managed marketing and new product development for Häagen-Dazs, Green Giant, Yoplait, and Cheerios while at Nestlé and General Mills.

Before my brand life, I developed web sites at an interactive agency called iXL, was a wine steward on a Wyoming dude ranch, and sold advertising for the first English language magazine in Prague.

I currently live in Richmond-upon-Thames on the outskirts of London with my wife and two daughters.